Flowers Speak

REV. LORRAINE APLIN

Hardcover: 978-1-961438-29-3
Paperback: 978-1-959224-94-5
eBook: 978-1-959224-95-2
Library of Congress Control Number: 2023908311

Ordering Information:

Prime Seven Media
518 Landmann St.
Tomah City, WI 54660

Printed in the United States of America

Acknowledgements

I would like to thank the energy of flowers for their wonderful message to the people of Earth and to my dear friend of many years, Jan Hardisty for letting me have the run of her garden with the camera in hand. A big thank you to Steve Harris and Prime Seven Media for the wonderful help in putting this book together.

We, the flowers of planet earth, wish to bring a message
to the people of earth.

With one voice and one

heart we come

with love.

All life is a manifestation

of the Great Spirit

be it plant,

mineral,

animal,

or human.

The body is a temple
and therefore divine,
and thus needs
to be honored.

Honored with good food, and
water, also and importantly
physical and
spiritual exercise.

As a spiritual being your
understanding of the power
of thought
is very important.

Have you not understood
the saying
"as a man thinketh so he becomes"

The one known as
Jesus, the Christed One, spoke
of seeing a glass half full or half empty.

This dear ones, is about
your thoughts being on the side of negativity or as being positive.

It is important to understand the
message
here.

Your thoughts are powerful
and they shape your life.

Think positively about
the way you would like your life journey to move forward.

Visualise your dreams positively
and do not dwell on reasons you think that they cannot come true.

You look around your
world and see trouble and strife, war and riots.

Do you think, as many do, that
these things just Happen?
Do you believe that strife comes about as a result of bad luck?

Personally and or collectively
negative thoughts collect
themselves together
into a dark mass which 'dumps'
itself into your lap so to speak.

It is time to wake up
and become one with
the power that you are.

Become a walking talking connection to the Divine.

On earth.

Here.

Now.

All have had many lives that,
before coming into each incarnation, have sworn to live by the Law,
Universal Law, from which many
religious groups have taken
their teachings.

Many souls claim allegiance to one religion or another,
and have done so for thousands of years.

Why then is there so little peace on earth?

The answer is simple.

There is not enough LOVE.

It is not religion people need
to understand, but
Spiritual Law.

For you all live, breathe and exist
within this law.

There is a very ancient
saying,
"man know thyself, then thou will
know God and the universe".

Life has become very busy, people rushing this way
and that, and mostly getting nowhere.

So many are feeling that
something is missing in
their life,
and
not aware that the missing piece is their connection
to the spirit within.

It is time to stop, take a
breath, smell the flowers,
attune yourself to the Divine,
the God force within
each and
every one of you.

Meditate and align
yourself to the Light
within, the Light of your being, of your existence.

This is where you will
receive
your connection.

Your guidance.

Your support.

Your protection.

This is where you will know that
you are all one,
that there is, in truth,
no separation.

Not alone but 'all one'.

All are under 'GOD', the
Divine Connection,
the Great Spirit,
Creator of all that is.

As is all of creation.

There
are many different
conceptions of what God is,
and is not.

Some say there is only
one name to call upon God, and, their way is the only way of praying.

This is not so.
Your thoughts and prayers
must come from the
Heart.

Be heartfelt, sincere.

Prayer, said for the sake of doing so,
without sincerity,
without feeling, achieves little.

The purpose of all
souls are to become
Christ Like.

Souls who have attained
70% or more love
are referred to as
Ascended Masters, be they male or female,
and need not return to
earth unless they
choose to do so.

Many of these ascended beings
do come to earth again, out of love
for their brothers and sisters.

They come to teach, to inspire,
as Jesus did,
to bring messages from angels,
spirit guides and
other beings of Light.

Bringing teachings and guidelines of how to live in harmony
with all life on earth.

For it is only this way that there
will be peace for one and all.

Nurture yourselves by living with
Love.

Develope the art of appreciation.

Feel gratitude for the beauty of all life on earth.

Smile.

Touch lovingly.

Love heals and you all crave
Love and healing.

Want to go to paradise when you die?

We tell you now,
that where you end up on the
"other side",
depends on your love quotient.

That is, how well you have
lived lovingly.

Human kind can
deceive themselves into
believing that lies are
truth,
but cannot deceive
the Angelic ones or their own
spirit,
or
manipulate Universal Law.

All beings on planet earth
are subject to the
same
Universal Laws
regardless of their
station in life.

Lay not a hand
on anyone in anger,
nor seek to hurt
another
in any way as anger,
like love
comes back
to you.

Understand that every
thought,
every feeling,
every deed you do, is an action
that goes out from you
and therefore comes back
in like kind.

Do not wait for others
to step forward first.
Take your step forward, for
none other
can do it for you, or heal you.

Your healing comes from
within, from living
in truth, love and light, from being caring, and reaching out to others.
Start now.

Stop the struggle.

It gets easier after the first step.

Remember,
you are doing it for yourself.

Each of you have at least
two guides
and as you grow in spirit
other helpers
are able to draw near.

They are always beside you.

But you must ask.

They are waiting.

There are healing angels

in every room

where they are needed.

Wherever there are sick and injured ones,

these healing angels are bringing support and comfort.

Ask for their help, and their guidance for it is their joy to assist.

Be grateful for your time on
planet earth,
and the lessons you learn,
for this is your chance
to step off the
wheel of rebirth.

Look at the flowers and marvel
at their beauty.
Let your heart swell
with love, appreciation
and gratitude.

There is so much diversity,
so many shapes, sizes, colour and purfumes.
So much beauty.

Take a moment often to be still, picture your favorite flower,
breathe in the perfume,
ask for guidance and give thanks to that which you conceive to be the
highest and Best.

Think of yourself as a flower
unfolding under the hand
of Divine Spirit.

Look around you, see the beauty everywhere, breathe in joy, breathe out peace, and
let your heart energy expand.

Look at the children and let
your heart glow with love.

We thank the Great Light of all creation for this opportunity
to speak
to bring this message
to you.

May all be touched by the Spirit of all life flowing through their being.

Amen.

*All photos in this book were taken by the author
in many different areas of Australia.
Many are natives that some readers may not have seen before.*